Form Of Return: On An Uniform System Of Accounts And Returns

Committee Of Railroad Commissioners

In the interest of creating a more extensive selection of rare historical book reprints, we have chosen to reproduce this title even though it may possibly have occasional imperfections such as missing and blurred pages, missing text, poor pictures, markings, dark backgrounds and other reproduction issues beyond our control. Because this work is culturally important, we have made it available as a part of our commitment to protecting, preserving and promoting the world's literature. Thank you for your understanding.

FORM OF RETURN,

AS ADOPTED BY THE

"Committee of railroad Commissioners and Accountants,"

ON AN

UNIFORM SYSTEM OF ACCOUNTS AND RETURNS,

AT A MEETING HELD APRIL 24, 1879;

TOGETHER WITH

A FORM FOR DIVISION OF OPERATING EXPENSES,

AS PROPOSED.

BOSTON:
PRINTED BY RAND, AVERY, & COMPANY,
117 FRANKLIN STREET.
1879.

BOSTON, May 20, 1879.

TO THE RAILROAD COMMISSIONERS OF THE VARIOUS STATES.

Gentlemen, — I have been instructed by the Committee on Uniform System of Accounts and Returns to forward to you the Rules and form of Return, adopted by them at a meeting of the Committee with the Railroad Accountants. The form for division of operating expenses was left for future consideration, and will come up for discussion and decision (together with the form adopted) at the general convention of Railroad Commissioners, to be held at Saratoga, the 10th of June next. A form for the division of operating expenses, as submitted by Mr. Towne, is herewith also included. As in all probability *some* form of return will be adopted at the convention, and hereafter used by the various commissions, it is important that it should be one that will meet the requirements with as few objectionable features as possible: any objections therefore to the form adopted by the committee, will have to be brought up at that time.

Your attention is called to the enclosed, trusting that you will give it a careful examination, with a view to its adoption or rejection, in whole or in part, by the convention. I am very respectfully,

J. H. GOODSPEED,
Secretary, &c.

RULES, Etc.

A meeting of the committee of railroad commissioners and railroad accountants on "Uniform System of Accounts and Returns," appointed at the general convention of railroad commissioners in November last, was held at the St. Nicholas Hotel, New York City, Thursday, April 24, 1879, as per call of the Chairman, Mr. Woodruff of Connecticut. There were present of the committee, Messrs. Woodruff of Connecticut, Carter of Virginia, Turner of Wisconsin, railroad commissioners; Messrs. Leland of Ohio, Shinn of Pennsylvania, Wilbur of Boston, railroad accountants; and J. H. Goodspeed, secretary; also, by invitation, Gen. F. A. Walker, railroad commissioner of Connecticut, and Mr. George E. Towne, accountant, of Boston.

On a general discussion of the matter before the committee, it was unanimously voted, —

"That it is the sentiment of the committee, that the system of accounts and returns should include a showing in detail of the annual operation."

The following general rules, in regard to the manner of keeping accounts from which the returns are to be made, were discussed and adopted: —

I.

All liabilities (including interest accrued on funded debt) shall be entered upon the books in the month when they are incurred, without reference to date of payment.

II.

Expenses shall be charged each month with such supplies, materials, &c., as have been *used* during that month, without reference to the time when they were purchased or paid for.

No expenditure shall be charged to property accounts, except it be for actual increase in construction, equipments or

III.

other property, unless it is made on old work in such a way as to clearly increase the value of the property over and above the cost of renewing the original structures, &c.

In such cases, only the amount of increased cost shall be charged, and the amount allowed on account of the old work shall be stated.

IV.

Mileage of passenger and freight trains shall include only the miles shown to be run by distances between stations; allowances made to passenger or freight trains for switching, and all mileage of switching engines computed on a basis of ten miles per hour for the time of actual service, shall be stated separately.

V.

Season-ticket passengers shall be computed on the basis of twelve (12) passengers per week for the time of each ticket.

VI.

Local traffic shall include all passengers carried on local tickets, and all freight carried at local tariff or special local rates.

All other traffic shall be considered through.

The form of return upon which the reports are to be made to the commissioners was taken up and decided upon, with the exception of the division of operating expenses.

A form of division of operating expenses was submitted by Mr. Towne; and the secretary was instructed to send copies of the same, together with the rules and form adopted, to the different members of the committee, asking them to take it under consideration for discussion and final decision at the next meeting of the committee, to be held at the time of the general convention of railroad commissioners in June next.

The form of return as adopted by the committee is as follows: —

GENERAL EXHIBIT.

Total income . . . .
Total expense . . . .
Net income . . . .
Interest on funded debt . . . . .
    "   " unfunded " . . . . .
Rentals . . . .
Balance applicable to dividends . . . .
Dividends declared (per cent) . . . .
Balance for the year . . . . . .
Balance (profit and loss) last year . . . .
   Add or deduct various entries made during the year not included above (specifying same).
Balance (profit and loss) carried forward to next year .

CHARGES AND CREDITS TO PROPERTY DURING THE YEAR.

Construction and equipment (specifying same) . .
Other charges (specifying same) . . . . .
Total charges . . . .
Property sold or reduced in value (specifying same) .
Net addition (or reduction) for the year . . .

ANALYSIS OF EARNINGS AND EXPENSES.

Earnings:
From local passengers . . . .
  Through   " . . . .
  Express and extra baggage . . . . . .
  Mails . . . .
  Other sources, passenger department . . .
Total earnings passenger department . . . .
  Local freight . . . .
  Through freight . . . .
  Other sources, freight department . . . .
Total earnings, freight department . . . .
Total transportation earnings . . . . .
  Rents for use of road . . . .
  Income from other sources (specifying same) . .

     Total income from all sources . . . .

EXPENSES.

(See form submitted.)

ASSETS AND LIABILITIES.

Assets:
Construction account
Equipment   "
  (Locomotives, No.   )
  (Parlor and sleeping cars, No.   )
  (Passenger cars, No.   )
  (Baggage and mail cars, No.   )
  (Freight cars, No.   )
  (Other cars, No.   )
Other investments (specifying same)
Cash items:
  Cash
  Bills receivable
  Due from agents and companies
Other assets:
  Materials and supplies
  Sinking funds
  Debit balances

    Total assets

Liabilities:
Capital stock (as specified below)
Funded debt (as detailed below)
Unfunded debt, as follows:
  Interest unpaid
  Dividends unpaid
  Notes payable
  Vouchers and accounts
  Other liabilities
Profit and loss or income accounts

    Total liabilities

PRESENT OR CONTINGENT LIABILITIES NOT INCLUDED IN BALANCE-SHEET.

Bonds guaranteed by this company or a lien on its road
  (specifying same).
  Over-due interest on same .
  Other liabilities (specifying same)

MILEAGE, TRAFFIC, ETC.

Mileage passenger trains . . . . . .
   Freight   " . . . . . .
   Switching   " . . . . . .
   Other   " . . . . . .

      Total train mileage . . . . . .

Miles run by passenger, mail, and baggage cars (north or east) . . . .
Miles run by passenger, mail, and baggage cars (south or west) . . . .
Miles run by freight cars (north or east) . . .
  "   "   "   " (south or west) . . .
Number of season-ticket passengers . . . .
Number of local passengers (including season) . .
Number of through passengers . . . .
Total number of passengers carried . . .
Mileage of local passengers (north or east) . . .
  "   "   " (south or west) . . .
Mileage of through passengers (north or east) . .
  "   "   " (south or west) . .

      Total passenger mileage . . . . .

Number tons local freight carried . . . .
Number tons through "   " . . . . .

      Total tons freight carried . . . . .

Mileage of local tonnage (north or east) . . .
  "   "   " (south or west) . . .
Mileage of through tonnage (north or east) . . .
  "   "   " (south or west) . . .

      Total freight mileage . . . . .

Average weight of passenger trains . . .
    "   number of cars in passenger trains . . .
    "   weight of freight trains . . . .
    "   number of cars in train . . . .
    "   number of persons employed . . .
Length of road, branches, sidings, &c. . . .
Names of officers and directors . . . .
Corporate name of company . . . . .

[FORM PROPOSED BY MR. GEORGE E. TOWNE.]

REPORT OF THE A B & C RAILROAD COMPANY FOR YEAR ENDING SEPT. 30, 1879.

GENERAL STATEMENT OF RESULTS.

Aggregate income	$1,050 000 00	
" expenses . . .	682,000 00	
Net income		$368,000 00
Accrued interest on funded debt .	160,000 00	
" " " floating debt .	10,000 00	
Taxes paid during the year . .	29,000 00	
Rentals leased lines, specifying same —		
D & E Railroad Co. . . .	18,000 00	
F & G Railroad Co. . . .	12,000 00	
		220,000 00
Balance applicable to dividends .	. . .	148,000 00
Dividends declared during the year as follows: —		
Dec. 28, 1879, 3 per cent; June 26, 1879, 3 per cent .		132,000 00
Balance to credit of Profit and Loss,	. . .	16,000 00
Profit and loss credit balance, Sept. 30, 1879	78,500 00	
Items added during year, specifying same:		
	300 00	
	600 00	
		79,400 00
		95,400 00
Losses from bad debts during year,	1,200 00	
Other debit items, specifying same:		
	700 00	
	400 00	
		2,300 00
Balance carried forward . .	. . .	93,100 00

DETAILED STATEMENT OF INCOME AND EXPENSES.

Income.

	Passenger Trains.	Freight Trains	Miscellaneous.
Transportation through freight and passengers,	$290,000 00	$300,000 00	—
Transportation local freight and passengers,	150,000 00	265,000 00	—
Transportation mails	10,000 00	—	—
Transportation express and extra baggage	15,000 00	—	—
Rents	—	—	$10,000 00
Miscellaneous	3,000 00	1,000 00	6,000 00
Aggregate income	468,000 00	566,000 00	16,000 00
Train mileage	350,000 ms.	280,000 ms.	10,000 ms. other. 125,000 ms. switching.

Group A, showing Train Movement Service.

Expenses.

	Construction.	Switching.	Passenger.	Freight.
Locomotive Department,—				
1. Repairs	$600 00	$5,700 00	$16,000 00	$12,700 00
2. Fuel	1,500 00	13,500 00	37,500 00	37,500 00
3. Oil and waste,	150 00	1,200 00	3,400 00	2,750 00
4. Water	50 00	250 00	1,000 00	700 00
5. Engineers and asst's	900 00	8,300 00	26,200 00	21,500 00
6. Miscellaneous	50 00	500 00	1,400 00	1,150 00
Total	$3,250 00 Carried to Group C.	$29,450 00 Carried to Group B.	$85,500 00	$76,300 00
Car Department,—				
7. Repairs			$25,000 00	$40,000 00
8. Mileage			2,000 00	18,000 00
9. Train-men			24,000 00	31,000 00
10. Fuel, oil, and waste			2,100 00	1,900 00
11. Miscellaneous			5,000 00	3,000 00
Total			$58,100 00	$93,900 00
Wear of Track,—				
12. Iron laid, —— tons, —— miles			$2,000 00	$3,000 00
13. Steel laid " "			12,000 00	18,000 00
14. Repairs track			12,000 00	18,000 00
Total			$26,000 00	$39,000 00

Recapitulation Group A.

	Per Mile.	Passenger.	Per Mile.	Freight.
Locomotive Department	.244	$85,500 00	.272	$76,300 00
Car Department	.166	58,100 00	.335	93,900 00
Wear of Track	.074	26,000 00	.140	39,000 00
Aggregate cost of moving trains	.484	$169,600 00	.747	$209,200 00

Mem.—Cost of switching, construction and other trains, included in Groups B and C.

GROUP B, SHOWING STATION AND DEPARTMENT SERVICE.

	PASSENGER.	FREIGHT.
Department, Office, and Station Expenses: —		
15. Station and office men	$24,000 00	$56,000 00
16. Station and office bills, fuel and supplies	7,000 00	13,000 00
17. Telegraph expenses	3,300 00	2,700 00
18. Switch, flag, and signal men,	14,000 00	11,000 00
19. Switching engines	2,600 00	26,850 00
Total	$50,900 00	$109,550 00
Miscellaneous: —		
20. Removals snow and ice	$850 00	$650 00
21. Losses, damages, and gratuities	1,000 00	1,000 00
22. Spark insurance and losses	550 00	450 00
Total	$2,400 00	$2,100 00

Recapitulation Group B.

	PER MILE.	PASSENGER.	PER MILE.	FREIGHT.
Office and station expenses	. .	$50,900 00	. .	$109,550 00
Miscellaneous	. .	2,400 00	. .	2,100 00
Total operating expenses other than those of trains	.152	$53,300 00	.399	$111,650 00

GROUP C, SHOWING MAINTENANCE AND GENERAL MANAGEMENT.

Maintenance of Property.

23. Repairs of road and road-bed	$37,000 00
24. Repairs of bridges	15,000 00
25. Repairs of buildings	20,000 00
26. Repairs of fences, signs, and crossings	6,250 00
27. Renewals of ties	20,000 00
Total	$98,250 00

Miscellaneous.

28. Watchmen	$7,000 00
29. Insurance and loss by fire	3,000 00
30. General expenses	30,000 00
Total	$40,000 00

Recapitulation Group C.

Maintenance of property	$98,250 00
Miscellaneous	40,000 00
Total maintenance and general management	$138,250 00

SUMMARY OF EARNINGS AND EXPENSES.

	PER MILE.	PASSENGER.	PER MILE.	FREIGHT.
Gross train income,	1.337	$468,000 00	2.022	$560,000 00
Cost of moving trains, Group A	.484	169,600 00	.747	209,200 00
Net train income after deducting train expenses	.853	$298,400 00	1.275	$356,800 00
Station and department service, Group B	.152	53,300 00	.399	111,650 00
Profits, freight and passenger departments	.701	$245,100 00	.876	$245,150 00

Profit freight department, brought down	$245,150 00
Profit passenger department, brought down	245,100 00
Miscellaneous income	16,000 00
	$506,250 00
Maintenance and general management, Group C	138,250 00
Net income for year	$368,000 00

INSTRUCTIONS TO ACCOMPANY THE SUGGESTED SYSTEM OF UNIFORM RETURNS FOR THE RAILROADS OF THE UNITED STATES.

The questions will be grouped as follows. The figures shown in answer, computations being in all cases made conformably to the rules given, are intended to cover the various items, as specified under the headings herewith submitted:

INCOME.

See rule for line of division between "local" and "through" transportation. All income items to be reported, less deductions for rebates, over-charges, and refunds. Charges for carriage and service outside of trains, to be deducted from mail and express income, to be classified in the figure columns, under the three headings as designated.

Mem. — See rule upon the computation of train mileage.

EXPENSES.

Divided into three groups, A, B, and C, representing respectively, "Train Movement Service," "Station and Department Service," and "Maintenance and General Management."

GROUP A.

To include, under the three general headings of "Locomotive Department," "Car Department," and "Wear of Track," all the expenses which make up the cost of moving trains, and which in their volume, keep substantial pace with the reduction and increase of train mileage.

Locomotive Department.

To include every thing connected with expense of motive power; to be classified, in figure columns, under headings as designated, which refer to the use of locomotives in different classes of work. This, being the locomotive department, must include them all for convenience; but, for inclusion in expenses, the figures in column headed "Construction," being for gravel and similar trains, go into "Repairs of Road," Group C. The expense of switching engines belongs to Group B; leaving only the actual running, on passenger and freight trains, to be included in Group A.

1. *Repairs.* — To include materials used and labor performed in repairing locomotives and tenders; also, proportion of shop expenses. Classification under designated headings, on basis of general locomotive mileage.

2. *Fuel.* — To include cost, charges, preparation, and handling of all fuel used in locomotives. Classification on basis of use of each.

3. *Oil and Waste.* — To include cost of all used in lubricating and lighting locomotives. Classified on basis of use.

4. *Water.* — To include water purchased, wages paid to men and tools, supplies, oil and waste used at water stations; repairs of engines, wind-mills, pumps and machinery at stations. Classify on basis of mileage.

5. *Engineers and Assistants.* — To include wages of engineers, firemen, and wipers. Classify as employed, apportioning *pro rata* wipers and others not actually having stations upon the engines.

6. *Miscellaneous.* — To include tools and materials furnished to locomotives; fuel, oil, water, waste, and gas, to engine-houses; and all other items pertaining to locomotive department not elsewhere designated. Classify on basis of mileage.

End of Locomotive Department.

Car Department.

To include all train-movement expenses accruing behind the locomotive and above the rails.

7. *Repairs.* — To include all material used and labor performed in repairing passenger, baggage, mail, express, freight, and caboose cars; also proportion of shop expenses. Classify to freight or passenger trains, according to description of car.

8. *Mileage of Cars.* — To include excess of payments over receipts for use of cars. Classify according to description.

9. *Train-men.* — To include wages of conductors, baggage and brake men, examiners of running gear, and car-cleaners. Classify as employed.

10. *Fuel, Oil, and Waste.* — To include cost of what is used. Classify as used.

11. *Miscellaneous.* — To include checks, punches, tickets, tools, supplies, car seals and locks, and all materials pertaining to trains, not elsewhere specified. Classify as used.

End of Car Department.

Wear of Track.

To include all items of track-wear due to, or growing out of, the passage of trains.

12. *Renewals of Iron.* — To include cost of iron rails laid down, deducting the value of old rails taken up. Classify to freight and passenger trains, on the basis of mileage of each, adding thereto for this purpose the proportion of switching mileage pertaining to each.

13. *Renewals of Steel.* — To include cost of steel laid down, deducting the value of old rails taken up. Classify as directed for " Renewals of Iron."

14. *Repairs of Track.* — To include cost of joints, spikes, shims, bolts, nuts, and track tools; also labor laying ties and rails, and levelling track; also repairing rails and hand-cars, and repairs and renewals of frogs, switches, and guards; also in general all materials and labor not otherwise specified, and excepting the ties, expended upon the track above the ground. Classify as directed under " Renewals of Iron."

End of " Wear of Track " and "Group A."

GROUP B.

To include under general headings of "Department, Office, and Station Expenses," and "Miscellaneous," all transportation expenses not accruing directly from train movements. The items of this group refer rather to the terminal than to the hauling service; to the work *at* rather than *between* the stations. They are naturally divisible between freight and passenger departments.

Department, Office, and Station Expenses.

To include, as the heading implies, all expenses incurred in the stations and offices of the freight and passenger departments.

15. *Station and Office Men.* — To include salaries of general freight and passenger agents, assistants and clerks, of station agents and assistants, of freight-house and yard men, of foreign and travelling agents. Classify as employed.

Men. — At all stations where the agent, or any or all of the men, are employed jointly upon both freight and passenger business, classification of the wages should be made to the respective departments upon the basis of the proportionate earnings of each at that station. At all stations, however, classify direct to either department the wages of all who are in sole employ of either.

16. *Station and Office Bills, Fuel, and Supplies.* — To include furniture, fixtures, stationery, printing, and all supplies, cost of heating and lighting at stations and department offices. Classify as directed in the note under "Station and Office Men," directly, where possible; otherwise, by apportionment, on basis of earnings or business.

17. *Telegraph Expenses.* — To include salaries of superintendent and operators, chemicals, instruments and repairs of same, wages of line-men, and all materials for repairs of line. Classify on basis of train mileage.

18. *Switch, Flag, and Signal Men.* — To include wages of men, oil, lights, flags, lanterns, switch locks and keys, switch frames, targets, signals, and all repairs of same. Classify

according to mileage, adding, for this purpose, switching to freight and passenger mileage proportionately.

19. *Switching Engines.* — To include figures brought down from locomotive department, column headed " Switching." Classify according to service.

Close of Department, Office, and Station Expenses.

Miscellaneous. — To include miscellaneous items of operating expenses other than those above specified.

20. *Removals of Snow and Ice.* — To include labor of men, expenses of engines with ploughs, repairs of ploughs, tools and materials furnished for the work. Classify on basis of passenger and freight mileage.

21. *Losses, Damages, and Gratuities.* — To include stock killed by trains, lost and damaged freight and baggage, passengers killed or injured, gratuities to employees injured, or the families of those killed; the expense of wrecking trains, damages to track and cost of repairing locomotives and cars injured by derailment, collision, or other accident. Classify to freight and passenger department, according to the class of trains upon which the damage was incurred.

22. *Spark Insurance and Losses.* — To include premiums on spark risks, where insured separately, and moneys paid for damages for fires set along the line in excess of receipts for insurance. Classify according to mileage of trains.

End of Group B.

GROUP C.

To include the cost of maintenance of that class of the property not affected in its wear and depreciation by train movements or department operations; also the cost of general management, belonging specially to neither of the departments. There being no natural basis for a division of these expenses, no classification will be attempted.

23. *Repairs of Road and Road-Bed.* — To include materials used and labor performed, ditching, ballasting, clearing weeds and bushes, building and extending side tracks, riprapping, changing location, repairing culverts and cattle-guards, expenses of engines for construction trains (see " Locomotive Department"), repairs of gravel-cars, and in

general all expenses incurred for repairing the waste and wear not accruing from the train movements. The stations of road-masters and of foremen, not included in wages of men, should be apportioned between "Repairs of Road" and "Repairs of Track," on basis of the aggregate cost of each for the year.

24. *Repairs of Bridges.* — To include materials used and all labor performed in repairing bridges, use or repair of pile-driver, and tools furnished.

25. *Repairs of Buildings.* — To include materials used and labor performed in repairs of all buildings, water-stations, platforms, wharves, turn-tables, and track-scales.

26 *Repairs of Fences, Signs, and Road-Crossings.* — To include all materials and labor expended in their repair.

27. *Removals of Ties.* — To include cost of ties.

28. *Watchmen.* — To include wages of watchmen, deducting for charge to other departments whatever special labor may be performed by them; also all lanterns, weapons, and appliances pertaining to watching, furnished them.

29. *Insurance, and Loss by Fire.* — To include cost of insurance premium, and all cost of restoring property in excess of insurance received. In case the property destroyed is replaced by a structure of greater value, a portion of the cost may be a proper subject for charge to construction, under the principle laid down in rule No. —.

30. *General Expenses.* — To include salaries of president, manager, superintendents, treasurer, auditor, cashier, paymaster, purchasing agent, and their respective clerks; stationery, printing, fuel and lights, rents, repairs, furniture and fixtures, expressage, stamps and postage of general office, salary or retainer of solicitor, and legal expenses; contributions for all railroad association expenses; subscription to periodicals, assessments for share of commissioners' expenses, and all other expenses of a general character not elsewhere specified.

End of Group C.

SUPPLEMENTARY.

A shop-expenses account should be kept, to include cost of fuel, oil and waste, and other supplies consumed at the repair-shops; for power, heating, and lighting; the salaries and wages of superintendents, engineers, and men whose labor is not applied directly to any work to which it can be classified; all travelling and other expenses of master mechanic and car-builder incurred in the service of the company. This account to be balanced monthly, quarterly, semi-annually, or annually, at pleasure; and the amount apportioned among the various repair accounts, *pro rata* to the contributions thereto, of the shop labor and materials.

SUMMARY OF INCOME AND EXPENSES.

Intended to give a comprehensive recapitulatory exhibit of the results, and the process of their attainment. Provision is made in special columns for showings per mile, as far as they have any propriety or value. A careful examination of the method of arrangement will suffice for a full understanding, without any detailed explanation.

Printed by Libri Plureos GmbH in Hamburg, Germany